THIS *Precious* MOMENT

The Wisdom of the Ba'al Shem Tov

RABBI BURT JACOBSON

Copyright © 2016 by Rabbi Burt Jacobson

All Rights Reserved

Published in the United States

ISBN 978-0-692-78830-1

Printed in the United States of America

Kehilla Community Synagogue
Piedmont, California

Cover photo by Burt Jacobson
Book design by Richard Miles

I dedicate this book to all the wonderful members of my congregation, Kehilla Community Synagogue, in Piedmont, California.

Special thanks go to my colleagues, the extraordinary spiritual leaders of Kehilla.

I also want to remember my friend, Susan Schacht, a member of Kehilla, who for many years acted as a writing coach and editor for my Ba'al Shem Tov writing.

CONTENTS

Introduction i
Chapter 1: This Precious Moment 1
Chapter 2: The Quest For Inner Freedom 9
Chapter 3: The Call To Transformation 17
Chapter 4: Of Love And Compassion 25
Chapter 5: Judging Others 35
Chapter 6: Radical Joy 43
Chapter 7: Sweetening Suffering 51
Chapter 8: Teacher Of Enlightenment 61
Conclusion 75
Acknowledgements 79

INTRODUCTION

The Jewish Renewal Movement has had a remarkable impact on American Judaism in recent decades. The principal founder of Jewish Renewal, Reb Zalman Schachter-Shalomi — may he rest in peace — sought to create a contemporary form of Jewish spirituality that would draw from past forms of Jewish religiosity and mysticism as well as present-day culture to fashion a new and revitalized Judaism for this era.

Reb Zalman was born in Poland, which was the birthplace of the eighteenth-century movement for Jewish spiritual renewal known as Hasidism. This widespread movement was initiated by a remarkable teacher, Israel ben Eliezer, known as the Ba'al Shem Tov (1700-1760). I once asked Reb Zalman about the influence of the Ba'al Shem on his life, and he told me, "If you were to remove every trace of the Ba'al Shem from my makeup, there would scarce be anything left of me!"

The earliest legends indicate that Israel ben Eliezer was born in Romania, the only child of a poor and elderly couple. When he was still an infant his parents moved to southeast Poland—what is now Ukraine—but the boy was orphaned soon after. Even as a child he lived the life of an outsider, spending time alone in the woods and studying the holy books in secret on his own. As an adolescent, he received a mystical manuscript from a mysterious Rabbi Adam, and the legends suggest that this gift began to transform the young man's vision. Israel's first wife, whom he married as an adolescent, died after only a year of marriage. His second wife, the daughter of a prominent rabbi, accompanied him to the Carpathian mountains, where the young man lived in seclusion as a hermit for many years.

In his late thirties Israel revealed himself to the Jewish public as an itinerant shamanic healer and wonder-worker, traveling to villages, towns and cities to ply his trade. In those years he became known as the Ba'al Shem Tov, which probably means the "Virtuous Master of the Holy Name," for we are told that he was able to use the Divine Name for magical and healing purposes. The Ba'al Shem is also known as the Besht, an acronym for <u>B</u>a'al <u>SH</u>em <u>T</u>ov.

But the Ba'al Shem also revealed himself to a community of kabbalists as a mystic and profound spiritual thinker and as a teacher who could guide his disciples toward enlightenment. His fame grew and in his early forties he settled in the town of Medzhibozh in the province of Podolia. His charismatic presence attracted a number of well-educated rabbis and other communal leaders who formed a circle of disciples around him.

Hasidic literature portrays the Ba'al Shem Tov as a healer, miracle worker, nature mystic, spiritual teacher, saint and communal leader. The very presence of this man testifiably engendered wonderment, awe, and love in those who met him, and his followers were swept into his dynamic mystical orbit.

Throughout the two and a half centuries since his death, Hasidic rebbes and writers have spoken and written about the Ba'al Shem Tov as if his sixty years on earth had been a miracle. Many viewed the Besht's powers as supernatural. His teachings were seen as revelation, and some even thought of him as divine. "The Ba'al Shem Tov was a flame of fire that descended from Heaven in human form," said one rebbe. Another declared that the master had actually been an angel of God!

After his death his disciples, particularly Rabbi Dov Baer of Mezerich, began to build the movement that came to be known as Hasidism. Within a few decades the Besht's insights and the example of his life radically altered the face of Eastern European Jewry. Through two and a half centuries and despite the decimation of Polish Jewry during the Holocaust, Hasidism continued to flourish. The Besht's influence also spread beyond the borders of the Hasidic world, inspiring modern Jewish teachers like Martin Buber, Abraham Joshua Heschel and Zalman Schachter-Shalomi.

•

We can gain a sense of what the Ba'al Shem Tov introduced into the Jewish world from a poem composed by Melech Ravitch (1893-1976), one of the preeminent Yiddish writers of the twentieth century.

I know You're near.
In this I've never been wrong.

Now You're a melody I can barely hear,
the beginnings of a song that will disappear.
Now a glint of light flitting from leaf to leaf
in the dark summer woods.
Now a fine luminous thread
that glistens as it weaves its way
through a piece of silk.
Now a luminous flash
between the lines of print.

In this verse, taken from a longer poem titled "Certainty," Ravitch evokes the core spiritual insight of the Ba'al Shem Tov: the world is suffused with God's wondrous and awesome splendor. And because each and every moment is divine, the perceptive seeker can find its presence everywhere and anywhere—in a glint of light flitting from leaf to leaf, or in a luminous thread running through a piece of silk, or in an insight that occurs while reading a book.

Melech Ravitch was born in Galicia, a region that currently straddles the border between Poland and Ukraine. He was a modern Jew, more at home in the secular world than in Jewish traditionalism. Deeply bound up with Jewish culture, he saw himself as a citizen of the world, a poet beyond nationalism. Nonetheless, in this poem the reader can sense the abiding influence of Hasidism on his soul.

Hasidic tradition maintains that the Ba'al Shem Tov's continuous sense of God's immanent presence flowed out of the master's ecstatic devotional practice of mystical worship, during which he would surrender and submerge himself in the great

Oneness, leaving all that was dark and burdensome behind. During those precious moments, he realized that the *Shekhinah*, the divine presence, embraced and permeated everything—even those things that seemed bleak and trying: there was nothing that was not filled with divinity. When he returned to the ordinary world, the Besht would channel a powerful flow of spiritual energy that generated wonder, freedom, joy, love and compassion, renewing and transforming the lives of those he touched.

•

The Ba'al Shem Tov entered my consciousness in 1973, during an enormously challenging period of my life. I was unsure of my value as a human being, confused about the direction of my life, and not even sure that I wanted to remain a Jew. My bond with the Besht originated in an intense encounter with the writings about him by the great Jewish thinker and teacher Abraham Joshua Heschel, with whom I had studied at the Jewish Theological Seminary.

I was drawn to the Ba'al Shem's astonishment at the miraculous character of existence, his celebration of life through rapture and joy, his loving embrace of people and—perhaps most important of all—the glory of being human and being a Jew. Within a few years I took the Besht as my rebbe, my spiritual master, recognizing that he could be my most important spiritual guide as I sought to heal the wounds of my childhood and youth and fashion a fulfilling Jewish spiritual path for myself.

In the process of learning about the Ba'al Shem Tov, and experimenting with spiritual practices inspired by his life and teachings, I found my consciousness and my life transformed in powerful ways. Because of my own experience, I became convinced that in this difficult and challenging time, the Ba'al Shem's fiery spirit might have the power to kindle the souls of seekers who long to experience the Light of the Infinite flowing through all things. I believe that the Besht's legacy can open us to the marvels present in the natural world and in human life, and that his teachings can nourish the energies of rebirth in a time when so much is uncertain and shifting.

•

I conclude this introduction with the remaining verses of Melech Ravitch's poem, "Certainty."

> *No longer will I seek Your hidden dwelling*
> *groping my way on the paths and roads*
> *where once with a wounded heart*
> *I sought in vain, asking every beggar*
> *where You could be found.*
> *Silently, faithfully, in ecstasy,*
> *wherever I go I'll carry You within me,*
> *the inner knowledge and the outer proof*
> *that I'm alive within Your warp and woof.*

And when a beam of sunlight
plays upon a window pane,
or pigeons fly homeward in the rain,
or children dance in a circle of joy,
or someone sheds a tear for another's pain,
there I will say, "It's You."
And all that's dark and burdensome in me
will be submerged in You,
in You alone,
as when a crystal stream
consumes a stone.

My hope is that the teachings and insights found in and between the lines of print in this book will open you, dear reader, not only to an appreciation of the gifts of the Ba'al Shem Tov, but even more to the wonders hidden in each precious moment.

THIS PRECIOUS MOMENT

I have been involved with the visual arts, and most especially with nature and landscape photography, for much of my life. I can recall moments when I have gazed in silent wonder at the reflections of light in a pond of still water, or the twisting arms or roots of an ancient tree, or the delicate colors and forms of a flower, or the intricate patterns on an iron-colored rock. Setting up my tripod, I would carefully compose and frame the subject in my camera's viewfinder. As I squeezed the cable release, I felt as if I were capturing this image for myself, but in truth it was the image that had captured me, drawing me into the intensity of its beauty. In that brief instant my separate self would briefly disappear as I melted into the scene. Experiences like these generated my fascination with the mystical.

My visual sensibility was also shaped by my relationship with the Jewish blessing practice. By 1956, my second year of college, I had begun to study and practice traditional Judaism. I remember purchasing a bi-lingual orthodox *Siddur*, a prayerbook that contained the full range of Jewish liturgy. Thumbing through the volume, I came across a section titled, "Blessings for Various

Occasions." Here I found a series of short *b'rakhot* (blessings) formulated by the ancient rabbis, that focused on the wonders that occur in the context of everyday living. Each blessing began with the words, *Barukh Atah Adonai, Eloheynu Melekh ha'olam.* … "Blessed are You, Lord our God, Ruler of the universe…." The *b'rakhot* that really stood out for me were those that were to be recited when one sees a natural wonder: lightening, a rainbow, a shooting star, lofty mountains, large rivers, the ocean, beautiful creatures, fruit trees flowering in the spring. I was also strongly drawn to the blessings for sunrise and nightfall in the daily liturgy.

I loved this blessing practice. It was obviously fashioned to train the individual to look for moments of amazement, and to relate these instances of wonder and surprise to their single spiritual source through gratitude and praise. The blessing practice helped me understand that every subject I was moved to photograph represented an instance of divine grace.

I have spent a great deal of time contemplating the work of great nature and landscape photographers like Edward Weston, Ansel Adams, Wynn Bullock, Minor White, Paul Caponigro and Eliot Porter. In 1970 I was fortunate to be able to spend a week studying with Caponigro. Like Adams, Caponigro was a pianist as well as a photographer, and many of his black and white images exquisitely evoke the musicality and the numinosity of existence.

Paul Caponigro wrote the following about the intersection between photography and the spirit:

All that I have achieved are these dreams locked in silver. Through this work it was possible, if only for brief moments, to sense the thread which holds all things together. The world, the unity of force and movement, could be seen in nature—in a face, a stone, or a patch of sunlight. The subtle suggestions generated by configurations of cloud and stone, of shape and tone, made of the photograph a meeting place, from which to continue on an even more adventurous journey through a landscape of reflection, of introspection.

Paul Caponigro, *Landscape,* McGraw-Hill, 1975, p. 67

I had majored in English literature in college, and I found a similar spiritual sensibility in many of the poets who became dear to me—Whitman, Wordsworth, Yeats, and Rilke. In one his most reflective works, "Lines Composed a Few Miles Above Tintern Abbey," William Wordsworth writes:

> And I have felt
> A presence that disturbs me with the joy
> Of elevated thoughts; a sense sublime
> Of something far more deeply interfused,
> Whose dwelling is the light of setting suns,
> And the round ocean, and the living air,
> And the blue sky, and in the mind of man,
> A motion and a spirit, that impels
> All thinking things, all objects of all thought,
> And rolls through all things.

In the 1960s I experimented with psychedelics such as LSD. These encounters actually brought me to a mystical experience of reality, disclosing to me the presence of an incomprehensible unity underlying, flowing through and embracing all existence. In the wake of these experiences I turned to the writings of the Eastern mystics and found that the immanence of the Spirit in all things was a persistent theme in their writings, especially in Indian and Chinese mysticism. The emphasis in both the *Upanishads* and the *Tao Te Ching* was not on the external beauties of creation, but rather on the unseen creative source of reality that inhered in and radiated from the creations.

> Self is everywhere, shining forth from all beings, vaster than the vast, subtler than the most subtle, unreachable, yet nearer than breath, than heartbeat. Eye cannot see it, ear cannot hear it nor tongue utter it; only in deep absorption can the mind, grown pure and silent, merge with the formless truth. As soon as you find it, you are free; you have found yourself; you have solved the great riddle; your heart forever is at peace. Whole, you enter the Whole. Your personal self returns to its radiant, intimate, deathless source.
>
> *Mundakas Upanishad,* translated by Stephen Mitchell in *The Essence of Wisdom,* Broadway Books, N.Y., 1998, p. 85

It was this vision of wholeness, in large part, that eventually drew me to the teachings of Ba'al Shem Tov. Like the kabbalists before him, the Besht knew that the mystery and oneness he was pursuing existed in an ethereal realm at the core of the human soul and at the heart of the cosmos, and that it permeated all of reality. Most people—even those who believe that this oneness exists—are unable to experience this unity in a profound way, because the world of our ordinary, everyday lives is filled with division, struggle and evil. Cut off from our celestial Root, we live in suffering and confusion.

How, then, to learn to see God's presence (*Shekhinah*) everywhere? And how do we move our broken selves and this shattered world toward the wholeness of the higher unity? This, teaches the Besht, is one of the primary purposes of spiritual practice. The ecstatic mystical experience (*devekut*) that comes at the zenith of devotional practice opens the heart and mind through an expanded awareness that re-unifies the fragmentary nature of ordinary consciousness. This re-unification occurs within the consciousness and life of the mystic, but the Besht avers that as more and more adepts learn to engage in such re-unification practices (*yihudim*), the power of their collective attainments will pave the way for the messianic era, the time when all human beings will live with a recognition of the holy oneness that pervades all existence.

Here are a few of the Ba'al Shem's teachings on discovering the divinity within the world.

> *There are some people who seek God,*
> > *but they believe that the divine is very far away,*
> > *surrounded by many high walls.*
> *And when they fail in their search, they say,*
> *"I sought him, but found him not." (Song of Songs 3:1)*
> *Had they been wise, however,*

they would have known that
"There is no place devoid of the divine." (Tikkunei Zohar)

You can find the Spirit in everything!
You can find God everywhere!
Understand this:
When you discover divinity in any facet of reality,
>*and bind your consciousness to that portion of God,*
>*you are binding yourself to the All in all!*

What, really, is this rock
>*lying before you on the ground?*
What is its true essence?
Is it not the divinity that gave it form?
Is it not the Shekhinah herself?
And this flower—what really is it?
And you—who think and speak—
>*what really are you?*

The Ba'al Shem offers counsel to those who wish to experience the underlying divine energy that pulsates through reality. Stop hurtling through life. Breathe. Open your eyes to what is in front of you. Allow your intuition to penetrate the outer skin of things. Experience God's presence in the here and now.

>*Contemplate the many and varied creations of our world*
>>*with the depth of true inward vision.*
>*Be aware not only of their outward appearance,*

> *but also of the life force that flows through them.*
> *Then you will see in them nothing but the divine power*
> *that animates and energizes them,*
> *giving them their very being.*
> *This is a power which at all times and in every moment*
> *sustains their existence.*

There are people who have cultivated the ability to look beneath the surface of our earthly existence and experience the underlying forces that animate our world. Albert Einstein used mathematics to fathom the inner structure of the cosmos. But what he came to was deeper than a knowledge of material existence:

> Try and penetrate with our limited means the secrets of nature and you will find that, behind all the discernible concatenations, there remains something subtle, intangible and inexplicable. Veneration for this force beyond anything that we can comprehend is my religion. To that extent I am, in point of fact, religious.

In his final photographs, one of my favorite photographers, Wynn Bullock, attempted to represent the very forces that animate and sustain the universe. They are remarkable images. Bullock wrote that "what you see is real—but only on the particular level to which you've developed your sense of seeing. You can expand your reality by developing new ways of perceiving."

I know this is possible. I experienced it on LSD. But in my own attempts at training myself to look with wonder at the world, I discovered a somewhat different route. Most of the time I live in a state of ordinary consciousness. But I have learned how to open my awareness to the preciousness of what lies before me in the present moment and link it to the whole of existence and the mystery at its depths. In this way I am able to perceive the world with greater clarity, wisdom and non-attachment. In such a state I become open to wonder, to radical amazement, to gratitude, to compassion, to love, and to a recognition of the divinity of the world and existence.

> The Ba'al Shem Tov taught:
>
> *Oi! Oi!*
> *The world is full*
> > *of lights and mysteries--*
> > *all awesome and wondrous!*
> *But you place your tiny hand*
> > *before your eyes,*
> > *and hide yourself*
> > *from their radiance!*

The master taught his disciples how to lower their hands so they, too, could experience the radiance of those lights and mysteries. May he also teach us.

THE QUEST FOR INNER FREEDOM

Babies come into this world with a capacity for wonder, joy and love. Life is fresh, full of marvels, but as we grow up most of us lose this gift. Being an adult means confronting complexity, difficulty and constant demands. Such ongoing responsibility can exact a severe toll on our souls. The pressure of so-called "normal living" is constant, relentless. We may close down our awareness and forget the awesome and marvelous character of life. And we may lose sight of the vast spiritual potential that lies within us as well.

One of our greatest spiritual challenges, then, is finding an inner freedom that might allow us to experience the world as a wondrous miracle. The Irish poet, William Butler Yeats, called this the recovery of radical innocence. My teacher, Abraham Joshua Heschel, identified the truly free individual as one who "is not carried away by the streams of necessity, who is not enchained by processes, who is not enslaved to circumstance." And he defined inner freedom as *"spiritual ecstasy,* the state of being beyond all interests and selfishness. Inner freedom is a miracle of the soul." Spiritual masters around the world have called this process awakening or enlightenment or liberation.

I first experienced such inner freedom during a mystical experience I underwent in 1966. During my experience I ascended to a state of consciousness in which all my normal cares and anxieties simply lifted from my awareness. In turn an incredibly wondrous living energy began to pulsate through my body and awareness. My need for control, in fact, all of my psychological defenses slipped away. *My* concerns, *my* anxieties, *my* "I"—none of these mattered. As my sense of boundaries dissolved, I became a vast transparent center of awareness, totally open, accepting, loving and ecstatic. Being was an entirely blessed and holy state—indeed, the *only* state.

The world was incredibly awesome, beautiful, bountiful, good. There was a transparency and perfection to it all. Each thing was in its right place, as it was meant to be, and nothing was lacking. The realization came to awareness that what people called "evil" was really only a slim thread winding through this wholeness that was in its essence perfection. As the ascent continued, there were no things at all, nothing to speak of—only the intense rapture of mysterious Is-ness. Consciousness completely merged with cosmos.

This profound journey was occasioned by the use of a psychedelic, and eventually what I experienced would change the very course of my life. But at the time it did not actually alter the way I was living. Yet I wanted to change, to become freer, and so the question arose for me, "How could I change my life so that I might live in accord with the vision I had experienced?" This set me on the path to spiritual self-transformation.

Years later I discovered that the Ba'al Shem Tov would be able to assist me in my endeavor, for he himself underwent many experiences of expanded awareness, and he taught his disciples how to spiritually transform their lives. The Besht regularly experienced inner freedom through the exaltation he experienced during his mystical worship. He described to one disciple how his ego would expand to include the whole of knowable existence, and then dissolve into the totality of being.

One year, before Passover, I was studying the Besht's teachings about the Exodus and I discovered that he had incorporated his vision of inner freedom into his interpretation of the story. To the master, the ancient tale of liberation became a paradigm for individual liberation in the here and now.

> The Ba'al Shem Tov taught:
> *The exile and the liberation from Egypt:*
> *These events happened to our ancient forbears,*
> > *but they also occur to each of us in our lives today.*

The Ba'al Shem understood the events of the Exodus as symbols of an unfolding psychospiritual path that, consciously chosen by an individual, could free him or her from the enslavement of living with sorrow, melancholy, and narrow self-centeredness. This path could open the seeker to the liberating expansiveness of joy and enlightened consciousness.

While Jewish tradition maintained that the Jewish people as a whole would be liberated only with the coming of the messiah, the Besht asserted that it is possible for individual seekers to attain liberation now, before the messianic era.

> *Every human being is a small universe.*
> *Within each of us lie the secrets*
> > *of bondage to Egypt,*
> > *the liberation of Passover and the Exodus,*
> > *and the movement toward Sinai.*

Pharaoh enslaved the Israelites, and the bondage in Egypt was an excruciating experience. The people toiled in the blazing sun at the beck and call of the Pharaoh, building the store cities of Pithom and Rameses. This servitude had dire spiritual effects on their lives.

> *What is the true meaning of the bondage in Egypt?*
> *Just this: That the consciousness*
> > *of the Jewish people was in exile.*
> *The children of Israel had lost the truth*
> > *that all existence flows from the light of* Ain Sof,
> > *the Infinite.*

In another teaching to his disciples, the Ba'al Shem put this slightly differently:

> *The exile in Egypt occurred*
> > *because the people had lost their ability to perceive*
> > > *that the world has a single Creator,*
> > > *and that the universe is filled with divine splendor,*
> > > *and that each and every day*
> > > *the Creator is continually renewing creation.*

Sunk in forced servitude, the people had lost their sense of wonder, their connection with the vast mystery of the cosmos, their realization that divinity is pulsing through creation, and that life is a gift of divine grace. We, too, can experience such a loss of vision when we become completely identified with our egos and with the roles we play in our daily lives.

But to be in exile is not only to be driven by the demands of the outer world. For the Besht, even more insidious is the subjugation to forces within ourselves, what the tradition calls the *yetzer ha'rah*, the "evil inclination." To the Besht this meant addiction to one's self-serving drives and desires. For the Ba'al Shem, living in Egypt/*Mitzrayim* ("narrowness") means being chained to narrowed consciousness, and being ruled by the tyranny of Pharaoh, the *yetzer ha'rah*.

How then to loose our chains? How to become free? When the body is sick, it requires a physician for healing; likewise, says the Ba'al Shem, when the spirit becomes attenuated, we require someone who can connect us to our concealed holiness and wholeness, teaching us how to bring these qualities into our conscious lives.

We cannot accomplish this on our own, the Besht tells us, because we have forgotten who we really are. For liberation to occur, the Israelites required an exceptional spiritual master, a *tzaddik* who had developed and deepened his own consciousness to such an extent that he was able to link every Jew of his generation to their original spiritual rooting--to enable them to find their way to the divine at their core and the particular spiritual destiny that awaited each of them.

In the Besht's reading of the Exodus story, Moses becomes the prototype of the enlightened spiritual master who dispels the fog of forgetfulness represented by Pharaoh, the *yetzer ha'rah*.

> *Then Moses arrived in Egypt, and by the miracles*
> *he performed it became known that indeed*
> *here is a Creator who interacts with the world,*
> *and that there is a divine plan, an underlying meaning*
> *to it all, both on the larger historical plane,*
> *and in each of the minute particulars of our lives.*
> *And this meaning is present in each and every step*
> *that one takes, and through every word that one utters.*

Moses' function as a spiritual teacher was to show each member of his people how to go within and liberate their consciousness from the domination of the Pharaoh inside themselves. In this way Moses countered their lack of faith.

What was Moses' talent? What gave him the ability to transform his generation in such a profound way?

The fully developed individual, one who possesses
 a clear knowledgeable consciousness, is able to link
 all the levels of his generation, and raise them up,
 uniting them to their Root, and uniting himself with them.
Such a person is called Moses.
He contains within himself his entire generation.
He is called Consciousness, *and his generation*
 is called the Conscious Generation.
But the wrongdoer is immature,
 and does not experience such awareness.

Moses was the personification of divine consciousness
 for his generation.
When he revealed himself to the world, forgetfulness departed.

What did Moses do to help individuals discover freedom and enlightenment? The first task on the road to inner freedom is the recognition that until now we have been on the wrong path. As a result of Moses' prodding, the people woke up and saw just how constricted they had allowed their lives to become.

Then the Shekhinah was revealed to the people,
 and they became aware
 that the divine is hiding in all reality.

We need teachers to help us on our journey toward inner freedom. The great Sufi poet, Jalaluddin Rumi, wrote: "Whoever travels without a guide needs two hundred years for a two-day journey." But the outer teacher is only effective because each of us has an innate capacity for awakening to inner freedom. The Besht put it this way:

> *Every person is a microcosm embodying*
> *Moses and Aaron as well as Egypt.*

You have the power and depth of Moses within you. But from my experience you can only cultivate that potential with the help of a wise and skillful teacher who exemplifies the traits that you seek to develop.

There are certain rare spiritual exemplars—like the Buddha or Jesus or Lao Tze or Rumi or the Ba'al Shem Tov—whose personalities shine through the stories of their lives and whose teachings are so potent that they can inspire, guide and shape seekers in later generations, even though they themselves no longer live on the physical plane. For over forty years the Ba'al Shem has been such a master to me, and his path has helped me discover and bring to the surface the Moses-spark within myself.

THE CALL TO TRANSFORMATION

In the tales told about the Ba'al Shem, he is frequently pictured as a saint. He comforts people who are suffering, he cares for the poor and he is extremely charitable. He champions the cause of widows and orphans and he is concerned with people's livelihoods. He's willing to sacrifice himself for the welfare of others. The storytellers picture the Besht as a man who possesses knowledge, wisdom and good judgment. Though he is fully dedicated to his life purpose, he exhibits ecstasy, joy and humor. He knows quite clearly how he is to serve God and people and he accomplishes this in a fearless manner, but he also has a sense of modesty and humility.

This is how later Hasidim portray the founder of Hasidism, and the image is based on many early sources. And this is how he's still pictured today in popular literature. This is the Besht I fell in love with more than forty years ago.

But as I read more and more stories about him, I discovered that this depiction of the Besht was simplistic and idealized, for there are also early tales about the Besht that portray him in a rather negative light. These stories reveal that the Besht had three major character flaws. First, he was solitary and he resented being with people. Second, he was prone to violent temper tantrums, and his anger fell upon people who didn't deserve it. And third, the Besht could exhibit a bloated sense of grandiosity because he was keenly aware of his extraordinary talents and gifts.

When I first read these vexing stories about the Besht's harsher side, I was both shocked and puzzled. How could this man have been considered a saint if he exhibited such blatant character defects? Well, I brooded over this question for a long time. And then one day I experienced a sudden insight. It occurred to me that a person like the Besht could not have been a traditional Jew in eighteenth century Poland and not be aware of the importance and necessity of *teshuvah*—the call to moral and spiritual transformation.

Now if this were true, then the Besht must have been aware of his failings, and of course he would have made a great effort to transform his character. At the time I was not aware of any stories or teachings that spoke directly about the Besht's struggles to change his life. Nevertheless, I speculated that maybe the stories about the Besht's saintliness were evidence that the master had succeeded in transforming his negative character traits. This was, of course, a conjecture, but the more I considered it, the more plausible it seemed to me. I then turned to the tales about the Besht's life and to his teachings for confirmation of my theory.

The Hebrew word *ga'avah* can be translated as pride or vanity or self-inflation or grandiosity. The Besht taught a great deal about *ga'avah*. He said that *ga'avah* cuts us off from God, and that such self-worship is equivalent to idolatry. Moreover, the Besht asserts that *ga'avah* is even worse than particular transgressions. And he also quoted the teaching from the Talmud that anger is a form of *ga'avah*. All this indicated to me that the Besht knew just how serious his issues actually were.

Many of the insights attributed to the Besht have to do with *teshuvah*, with transformation. In his teachings, the Besht talks about the necessity for actively struggling against one's regressive traits. I believe that these insights derive from the master's own struggle with the dark forces in himself. His teachings about pride, anger and *teshuvah* then, may have been warnings to his disciples that they were not to imitate his negative traits. Rather, they were to emulate his attempts at transforming his shadow side.

The Besht often speaks about the need to cultivate humility as a remedy for pride. He taught that rather than projecting our negative traits onto others, individuals must stay mindful of their shortcomings, continually struggling to change and grow.

There is a striking legend that describes how the Ba'al Shem learned to be a *hasid*, a person who loved God completely and loved all of God's creatures. Somehow the Besht understood that he could learn the secret of becoming a true *hasid* from Satan and he magically summoned the dark angel to this world. Satan appeared to the Besht in the guise of a large black dog, and he was quite angry. "How is it that you, a mere human being, did not fear to bring me to this lowly world? I seldom wish to descend. My work here on earth is accomplished by my myriad messengers."

"I do not fear you," answered the Besht. "I stand in awe of God alone."

"What is it you wish of me?" asked the irate angel.

"I want the keys to being a true *hasid*," the Besht said.

But Satan was furious and refused to reveal his secret, and he was about to return to heaven. Then the Besht gazed with great compassion at Satan. This changed the angel's demeanor and he gave the Besht the secret he had sought, whispering to him how to totally transform his lower nature.

Why would the Besht seek the key to becoming a *hasid* from Satan? In his wonderful book, *The Light and Fire of the Baal Shem Tov*, Yitzhak Buxbaum writes:

> The Rabbis teach that to achieve spiritual perfection a person must serve God not only with his good inclination, but with his bad side as well, turning all his evil tendencies to good uses, turning lust into divine love, anger at others into anger at one's lower nature, pride of self into pride at being a servant of God. The Besht sought this secret of transformation from the Satan, who is the outer manifestation of the inner evil inclination ...
>
> Yitzhak Buxbaum, *The Light and Fire of the Ba'al Shem Tov*, Continuum, 2005, pp. 98-99

Did the Ba'al Shem actually succeed in his efforts at *teshuvah*? Yes, to a great extent, but not completely. We see him slipping up again and again. He appears to have come to the conclusion that it would not be possible for him to reach perfection. On one occasion, we are told, the Besht's disciples asked him for permission to visit a famous spiritual master to observe him teaching. The Besht gave them his consent. Then they asked him how they would be able to discern whether this man was a true teacher or not. The Ba'al Shem said to them:

> *"Ask him how to get rid of pride and arrogance. If he gives you advice about this, you'll know that he's a fake. But if he answers, 'God help us, there's no advice for this!' then he's a true tzaddik, because one must struggle with pride one's whole life." The Ba'al Shem Tov constantly prayed to be saved from pride.*

Another tradition has it that on his deathbed, the Besht was heard to cry out

> *O vanity, vanity—even at this hour of my death you dare to approach me with your temptations, saying, "Look, Israel, what a great funeral procession you're going to have because you've been so good and wise." O vanity, vanity—away with you!*

In light of these revelations about the Besht's life we have to ask ourselves: what really is a *tsaddik*, a saint? Saints and spiritual teachers in every religious tradition exhibit a shadow side. They become saintly precisely because they recognize and struggle with their negative traits and work to transform them. "For the wonderful thing about saints," writes Phyllis McGinly, "is that they are *human*. They lost their tempers, got hungry, scolded God, were egotistical or testy or impatient in their turns, made mistakes and regretted them. Still, they went on doggedly blundering toward heaven." And religious novelist Frederick Buechner wrote: "A saint is a life-giver. I hadn't known that. A saint is a human being with the same hang-ups and dark secrets and abysses as the rest of us. But if a saint touches your life, you come alive in a new way."

One thing that I myself knew for certain: the Ba'al Shem had enabled me personally to come alive in a new way.

What was it that motivated the Besht to engage in *teshuvah*? We don't really know, but here too I have my conjectures. I believe that his desire to transform his life must have come from his early and sporadic experiences of inner freedom. Perhaps he asked himself (or God, or his inner spirit guide, Ahijah the Shilonite) how can I really become completely free? Somehow he learned that he would have to turn his life around rather completely, transforming his negative traits into positive virtues. And as he dedicated his life to serving God and people, his egocentric concerns became less important.

There are three lessons about *teshuvah* that I take from the Besht's life story. First, the need to look more deeply at my own flaws; second, the need to learn to accept myself with all of my flaws; and third, the necessity to cultivate greater humility.

I end this chapter with a reflection on the crucial importance of personal transformation for society at large. Raised as an orthodox *hasid*, Shulem Deen left the world of traditional observance. Nevertheless, he did not forsake his understanding of the necessity for personal transformation:

> ... we wage fewer wars today, and commit less violence, but we're also more savagely self-absorbed. We recognize many more rights for the historically marginalized, but we also feel more entitled than ever. We fight passionately for justice, but earnest individual self-reflection strikes us as precious. We are passionate about changing the world, but hardly so passionate about changing ourselves ... . Everyday acts of kindness seem so rare, the shaky phone videos of them go viral. We suddenly remember how good it feels to have our hearts warmed. A man lets another man sleep on his shoulder, and the world stands stunned.
>
> "Why This Month of Av Should Transform Us," in *The Forward,* August 19, 2016, pp. 46-47

It is my impression that many, if not most, political and social leaders do not engage in self-reflection and the inner work of self-transformation. This accounts for the addiction to power that so may leaders exhibit. Such unconscious "leadership" represents an appalling danger to the societies or organizations that these people purport to lead.

Jewish religious leaders will often speak about *tikkun olam*, healing and transforming the world, as the essence of Judaism. The Ba'al Shem Tov, however, taught that *tikkun ha'nefesh*, the transformation of the individual soul, is a prerequisite to *tikkun olam*. He was convinced that because every individual possesses a godly soul, carved from the divine essence of the world, we each carry a spark of the messiah. When we purify our lives, we come to realize the sacred depths within us. It is then that we can truly contribute to world transformation.

OF LOVE AND COMPASSION

One evening the Ba'al Shem Tov was walking home from the synagogue with one of his disciples, and he saw a drunken man staggering about the road, mumbling and singing a sad song. The Besht stopped and listened attentively. His disciple paused as well, but the young man stared as much at his master as he did at the drunken man.

Later the disciple asked his master why he had paid such close attention to such a man. "When a person bares his heart," answered the Besht, "it makes no difference how he does it. You must open your heart and listen. You cannot turn away."

Because divinity can be found everywhere, it can be found in every human voice no matter what the circumstances. The Ba'al Shem taught:

> *When you are truly attentive to someone who is speaking, listening to the inner depth of that person's words, you will hear none other than the voice of God, which gives life and being to the outer voice that you are hearing.*

The Besht's teachings on radical love, generosity and compassion were central to his worldview and to the way that he lived his life.

> *The Ba'al Shem once told his disciples:*
> *The life force of a human being is love.*
> *If you are truly aware, then you will understand*
> > *that love is among the highest of human virtues,*
> > *illuminating our existence like a precious jewel.*

Both the Bible and later Jewish tradition emphasized the importance of lovingkindness, but life in Poland before the time of the Besht had become harsh and grim, and love, sympathy and generosity were in short supply. A half-century before the Ba'al Shem's birth there had been a series of pogroms and tens of thousands of Jews had been slaughtered. In the years after being so brutally victimized, it would seem that politically powerless Jews vented their frustration and anger against one another. Jewish religion offered a measure of solace to the scholars, who had time to immerse themselves in the Talmud or the Kabbalah, but for the majority of ordinary Jews, who had to work for a living, Judaism offered little comfort.

Rabbi Ya'akov Yosef of Polonoye, one of the two most important disciples of the Ba'al Shem Tov, observed that among the Jewish masses there was a great deal of baseless hatred, rote observance of tradition, and a lack of spiritual inwardness. And he wrote that the Torah scholars were of no help. He characterized them as elitists pursuing their studies without true reverence for God, seeking only personal aggrandizement. The scholars studiously separated themselves from the common folk, and the people, in turn, had little or no respect for them.

Central to the Ba'al Shem's mission, then, was healing the brokenness of Jewish society. He and the other early Hasidic rebbes introduced a fresh understanding of joy, love and caring into eighteenth century Jewish life. They sought to bridge the divide between the spiritual leadership and the masses.

Hasidic tradition is filled with tales that describe the Besht as an extraordinarily loving, empathic, and compassionate human being. These stories can be extremely touching, at times even astonishing. It's probably impossible to know how many of these anecdotes and teachings—handed down with such warmth and love—go back to the master himself. Doubtless, some of them represent the storytellers' own longings for an ideal human exemplar of compassion and loving- kindness. But even the later, more romantic stories derive from the oldest traditions that depict the founder of Hasidism as a font of goodness, love, and healing.

In one moving story, a man comes to the Ba'al Shem and tells him that his son had broken away from Jewish tradition. "What should I do, Rebbe?" the suffering man asked. "Do you love your son?" the Besht asked. "Yes, I do," replied the man. "Then love him more," said the Besht.

Once, when he was teaching about the Golden Rule, "Love your fellow human being as yourself," (Lev. 19:18) the Besht interpreted the verse in the following way:

> *"Love your fellow human being because*
> > *he is exactly the same as yourself."*
> *Every Jew is rooted in the great Unity,*
> > *and at our depths we are all really one.*
> *So if you drive your fellow human being away,*
> > *you are only driving away your self!*
> *And this too:*
> *If you reject any part of the Unity,*
> > *you reject the Unity itself.*

Another time he related the verse, "Love your fellow human being as yourself," to the verse, "And you shall love the EverPresent, your Power, with all your heart, with all your soul, and with all of your passion," (Deut. 6:5) by teaching that the love of one's neighbor was a specific application of the love of God.

> *For when we love our fellow human beings as ourselves,*
> > *we actually love the Holy One,*
> > *because every person is part of God.*
> *What is it we are supposed to love in our fellow human beings?*
> > *Their essence, the divinity at their core.*

One of my favorite stories about the Besht's love and compassion is found in *Praises of the Besht*, the earliest collection of stories about the master. When the Ba'al Shem travelled from place to place as a healer, he was sometimes accompanied by his scribe, Tzvi Hirsch. It once happened that the Ba'al Shem and his scribe reached a certain city on a Friday afternoon. The people of the town knew that he was coming and they posted a messenger at the entrance to the city to inform the master where he was to stay as a guest over the Sabbath.

The Ba'al Shem and Hirsch went to the house, but when they arrived the householder's wife refused to receive them because their son was quite ill. The Besht and his scribe left to begin his healing work in the city. Later, however, he sent Hirsch to the house to inquire once again about lodging for the Sabbath. The householder's wife was disconcerted and said to the scribe: "How is it possible for both of you to stay here tonight? Can't you see that the boy is sick and I am in great sorrow." And then she cursed the Besht.

The householder did not dare interfere with his wife's decision, but he asked the scribe where he could find his master. When they located the Ba'al Shem, the householder placated him and told him that it was not possible for him to stay in his home, for it seemed like their child was dying. But the Ba'al Shem had been thinking about the boy and had made up his mind to cure him. He told the man that if he allowed them to stay the night, the boy would certainly live. The man agreed and the Besht and his scribe were received in the home.

The Ba'al Shem went immediately to bathe in the *mikvah* (the ritual bathhouse) to purify himself in honor of the Sabbath. There, using his inner spiritual sight, he perceived that the boy was quite feeble. When he returned to the house, he asked everyone to leave. The family members went to another house in the community for the Sabbath. Then the Besht ordered his scribe to leave as well. "Hirsch, I will call you when I need you to bring me the wine for the *kiddush*" (the blessing over wine to consecrate the Sabbath).

The Besht remained alone in the room with the boy. He prayed *Minhah* (the afternoon prayer service) next to the child, and he remained awake long into the night.

But Hirsch feared that the Besht might endanger himself by his intense efforts in praying for the sick boy, and so he returned to the house. He tiptoed to the door of the boy's room and slowly opened it, and he heard the Besht entreating the child's soul: "Enter this body! You must return to it because I cannot swear a false oath!"

The boy seemed like he had a little bit of life in him, but Hirsch could not discern whether he was dead or still alive. He left the house again, but after a short while he returned and entered the room. He found the Besht lying on the floor with his arms and legs stretched out. Then the master got up off of the floor and cried out loud: "Soul! Didn't I tell you to return to the boy's body? Why do you not listen to me?"

Seeing his scribe standing there, he shouted: "Hirsch, bring me wine for the *kiddush*." The Besht ate the Sabbath meal with Hirsch, and then the scribe left to go to sleep in another part of the house. But the Ba'al Shem stayed awake with the child the entire night, praying and entreating. By morning the danger had passed, and the Ba'al Shem gave the scribe instructions and medicines, and then went to pray at the synagogue.

The family returned to their home, and when the boy's mother saw that her child had recovered, she began to cry. The scribe heard her sobbing and he asked her:

"Why are you crying? My master succeeded in saving your son's life."

"How can I not cry after having cursed such a pious man?" she answered.

"Don't cry," he replied, "my rabbi is a good man and he will forgive you." Nonetheless, the woman continued to weep.

When the Ba'al Shem returned from synagogue, he heard the woman crying, but he did not approach her. He took Hirsch aside and asked him if he knew why the woman was sobbing. The scribe told him the reason for her tears. He bid his scribe speak to her:

"Tell her not to cry. She should prepare a good dinner for the third Sabbath meal. Tell her that I promise her that the boy will sit with us at the table." And so it happened.

This is how the story ends, but the narrator, sensing that his readers may be puzzled by some of the Besht's actions, goes on to explain that, in truth, the boy had been destined to die, but the Ba'al Shem refused to accept the verdict of Heaven. He pleaded for the child's life, and prayed that he live for more than sixty years, bear children, and earn a good living throughout his life. Because of the Ba'al Shem's psychic abilities, the boy's soul was compelled to reenter his body. But, the narrator adds, because the Ba'al Shem had countered the will of heaven, he knew and accepted the fact that he would have to be punished for his brazen deed. That is why he had lain on the floor with his hands and legs stretched out: to show his agreement that he would accept "fiery lashes" as a punishment for having made an oath to cure the boy.

That's how the narrative ends. And here is a second, related tale that illumines the meaning of the first story. Rabbi Dov Baer the Maggid of Mezeritch, once asked the holy Ba'al Shem Tov why he called those who followed his teachings *hasidim*, even those disciples who were no longer earnest and zealous. For the term "*hasid*," he said, should refer only to one who has attained the highest spiritual rung.

The master answered the Maggid by citing a particular Talmudic teaching from which he learned that

> ...*the core principle of Hasidism is this: One must love one's fellow human being and never harm him or her, even if this entails harming oneself. Thus love of the other takes precedence over love of oneself…. I have chosen to inculcate this virtue above all others into the hearts of my followers. And if you look deeply into their souls, you will detect at least a small part of this virtue in each of them.*

Jewish law and tradition would not require an individual to go to such altruistic lengths in his or her love for others, but the Besht believed that to be a true devotee of God one must act in accord with a principle higher than Jewish law, one which he believed came from God alone, and is the responsibility of the *hasid* to interpret and enact.

I'm not sure that I would be able to go to such lengths in my love for others. But as I have internalized the Besht's teachings over the years I have become increasingly aware of the loving presence of the divine flowing through all things. My life has been immensely affected by the example of the Besht's love of people, and I have worked to refine my own ability to love. This is true in my relationship with my wife, my friends, my colleagues, my students, and my congregants. I have been learning not only the path of loving other people, but also how to love myself in the same way that I love others. I, too, am part of Creation, and in loving myself I am loving one part of the divine.

I fail again and again, lost in self-preoccupation and forgetfulness. And nonetheless I believe that with God's help I continue to grow.

JUDGING OTHERS

As we learned in the last chapter, the Ba'al Shem Tov travelled from town to town in southeastern Poland offering his healing services to people with physical or psychic ailments. His reputation was widespread and wherever he would travel, people—Non-Jews as well as Jews—would flock to him for healing.

It happened that once while the Ba'al Shem Tov was on the road, he spent a few days in the town of Olyka. He knew the people in the town well, for Olyka was a regular stopover in his itinerary. The Besht was staying with Reb Menahem, a householder who was an elder in the community.

Now there was an itinerant preacher who had also come to Olyka, whose name was Reb Dovid HaMokhiakh, David the Chastiser, and it was his vocation to give sermons to the communities he visited. Like most of the traveling preachers, David the Chastiser would speak for two or three hours, and he would concentrate on the sins that he imagined the people he was speaking to had committed, imploring them to engage in *teshuvah*, self-transformation. The communities where Reb

Dovid spoke paid him a sum of money, and this was how he earned his living.

This was the first time that Reb David the Chastiser had come to Olyka, and he was going to preach at the synagogue on Shabbat afternoon, and of course all the men of the town would attend. Reb Menahem, the Ba'al Shem's host, invited him to go with him to the synagogue, but the Besht declined.

While the Ba'al Shem was waiting for his host to return home for the third Shabbat meal, a young man knocked on the front door. This man had been at the synagogue, listening to the preacher, and he was greatly perturbed. "Rebbe," he said, "David the Chastiser is vilifying all the people in the synagogue something terrible, telling them how awful they are and how they will burn in Hell for their sins!"

The Ba'al Shem became angry, but he knew there was nothing he could do to stop the sermon. So he told the man to return to the synagogue and ask his host, Reb Menahem, to return home immediately and not listen to the rest of the sermon.

So the man went back to the synagogue and spoke to Reb Menahem, and Reb Menachem left the synagogue to return home. But the man also whispered to a few other people that the Besht was really upset with the preacher. And when people heard that the Ba'al Shem was annoyed with David the Chastiser, they whispered this to those around them. One by one each of the townsfolk got up and slipped out of the synagogue, and soon there was no one left in the building except the preacher himself. Naturally, the man stopped preaching.

The preacher was terribly disheartened and the following day he came to the house where the Besht was staying and greeted the master, who was sitting in a chair. "And who are you, if I may ask?" the Besht inquired. "I'm David the Chastiser... Please tell me why you became angry with me yesterday?"

The Besht jumped up and tears poured from his eyes.

"Sir, you speak evil of the Jewish people. You only see what people are doing that is wrong and you instill guilt into their hearts. And you make them fear God by telling them that they will burn in Hell for their sins.

"Let me tell you something about one of the men in this town to whom you were preaching yesterday. Every day Reb Shlomo goes to the market to sell his vegetables and fruits. And he never earns enough to support his family. And so he stays in the market as late as he can, hoping to sell a few more items. But then he remembers that he is missing the afternoon prayers at the synagogue and he becomes anxious. 'Oy vey,' he says with a heartfelt cry. And so he takes a few minutes away from his vegetable stand and prays to God. And you know what, Reb Shlomo doesn't understand Hebrew. He doesn't know at all what he is saying, but he prays with so much longing and love for God that all the angels in heaven are stirred by his cries!"

The story ends abruptly. We don't know what happened next. We have no idea about how the preacher responded to the Ba'al Shem's reproof.

Was the Ba'al Shem angry with David the Chastiser? It certainly looks like it to me. And yet on another occasion the master taught that if you are going to reprove someone for a bad action they have done, you must do so with love for that person—or not at all. Maybe the Besht was taken by surprise at the appearance of David the Chastiser and simply lost his cool. Perhaps the Besht regained his composure and had compassion for the Chastiser. We will never know for sure.

I'm especially touched by the way that the Besht speaks about Reb Shlomo, how he knows the man's troubles. This is one of the ways in which Hasidic tradition depicts the Ba'al Shem's love for common people. I believe that the story about Reb Shlomo that he told the preacher was an attempt to evoke a change in Reb Dovid's heart, so that he would develop some compassion for the common people of Olyka.

The Besht is saying that we are not to judge our fellow human beings out of a sense of righteous morality, most especially when we know little or nothing about them. We are, instead, to love and embrace other people because they are embodiments of the divine.

Critical judgmentalism is pervasive in our society. So many of us tend to judge ourselves and others in negative ways. This one is better looking than me. That one is a conniver—better watch out! This one is dumb. That one is smarter than me—I'm jealous. How do I maintain my self-respect when I feel so weak in the presence of that one? This one is politically to the right of me—what a screwball! That one is politically to the left of me—what a simpleton! And on and on … . When such negative thoughts go through our minds, they keep us from empathy, from compassion, from love.

But the real spiritual question is what to do about these unfair judgments. How do we work with such thoughts when they pop into our heads? Well, the Ba'al Shem had a strategy.

First of all, the Ba'al Shem Tov taught that you can't prevent negative thoughts from cropping up in your mind. Maybe you're that rare person who doesn't have negative judgmental thoughts. If so, you are mighty lucky! Or perhaps you're highly developed spiritually and morally. But I must admit that I am personally not so fortunate or so developed. I have to cope with negative judgmental thoughts all the time.

So what does one do about these thoughts? The Ba'al Shem teaches that one should stay mindful and not identify with such thoughts. If you learn to stay aware and mindful, when judgmental thoughts arise in your mind look into them, see where they are coming from, and then let them go. You can choose to turn your awareness in a different direction. You can replace the negative thought with a positive thought. You can say inwardly: "That person, like me, is a spark of the divine." When you deliberately turn your awareness away from unfair judgmental thoughts toward the positive, you are engaged in a form of teshuvah.

And the Ba'al Shem had another related practice as well. He said that when a negative judgment arises in your mind about another person, turn that judgment back on yourself. Ask yourself: Where is that judgment coming from? Maybe I'm seeing a bad trait in this other person that is actually in me. And then, says the Besht, work on yourself to try to repair the flaw you have projected onto the other person. Wow! And the Ba'al Shem lived in the eighteenth century, long before Sigmund Freud and Carl Jung.

It seems to me that negative judgmentalism is one of the main impediments—perhaps the most problematic impediment—to compassion.

I shared an earlier draft of this chapter with Sandra Razieli, the director of Kehilla's Bar/Bat Mitzvah program and a spiritual leader in the congregation. Sandra offered me some valuable criticism of what I had written, much of which I've incorporated in this chapter. I'd like to share with you a few of her views on judgmentalism:

"I think the message of not being judgmental is dangerous to people who err on the side of too much compassion. They may hear the words 'be compassionate' and then think that they need to forgive and be understanding of behavior that is, in truth, unforgivable...."

And Sandra provided me with an example: "I recently spoke with a woman who has been in an abusive relationship for over forty years. She is financially secure and owns her own home. However, she is not able to leave the relationship because she feels she must be compassionate and understanding towards this man and it would be too hard for him if she leaves. She hasn't learned yet to be compassionate towards herself and the messages she received as a young girl and a woman about being loving and giving to others have blocked her from treating herself with compassion and respect."

I thank Sandra for this valuable insight. Not all judgments are negative and unfair. It is clear that without being able to make critical judgments, we would not be able to discern what is helpful or harmful, what is good and what is bad in particular situations. The real problem occurs when our judgments freeze into pervasive unconscious judgmentalism, because this habitual stance obscures our ability to be in connection with ourselves and with others.

Now a few words about anger. People get angry. The real question is how we act on that anger when we are annoyed or hurt. Do we simply lash out at those who make us angry? Or do we try to open a dialogue that might lead to constructive change?

I imagine that the Ba'al Shem would caution that in our anger we not lose our compassion for the victimizer as well as the victim. Something in the victimizer's past warped his or her humanity, but still this individual is a human being, made in God's image, with a *neshamah*, a pure Godly soul at their core. When we lose our ability to see divinity in any and every human being, we lose our connection with our own divinity, and our humanity as well.

RADICAL JOY

So. An old man is sitting in his house and he begins to complain: "Oy, am I thoisty! Oy, am I thoisty!" His granddaughter wanders into the room, hears him *kvetching* (complaining), goes to the kitchen and brings him a glass of water. The old man finishes the glass in one gulp. And then he says to his granddaughter, "Oy, was I thoisty!"

Why do we Jews seem to complain so much? Well, you may say, we are worldly people, and the world is in really bad shape. And there are some really ignorant and foul people out there running the show. Yes, yes, this is all true. But why is it that we worry so much about the condition of the world? And about the future? And about the Jewish people? Why has reading the newspaper—with all of its bad news—become a morning ritual for so many of us, more compelling than prayer? The answers to these questions require some digging around in Jewish history.

Until modern times we Jews had no power over our political destiny. We lived subject to the whims of those in power. And we were frightened by anti-Semitism—the Gentiles could always instigate a pogrom against us. We saw ourselves as victims. *Kvetching* was a response by Ashkenazi Jews to the conditions of the Exile that we were forced to endure century after century. And in a certain sense, *kvetching* became a kind of muted protest against those conditions.

Let me focus on one of those pogroms for a moment. In the year 1648, a Ukrainian peasant named Bogdan Chmielnitzky launched a revolt against the king of Poland and Lithuania and against the nobility. The Cossacks made common cause with Chmielnitzky's hordes, and their combined forces attacked nobles and Jews without discrimination. Tens of thousands of Jews were slaughtered in that massacre. You can imagine the trauma that the Jews of Poland experienced. On top of this, pious Jews believed that they themselves must have been the cause of these pogroms. Why would God punish them if they had done no wrong? So in response, many Jews became ascetics, fasting and mortifying their bodies to atone for their sins.

The Ba'al Shem was born fifty years later. And around 1736 he entered public life as a shamanic healer and spiritual teacher in the very geographical area where the Chmielnitsky pogroms had taken place. And one of the most important values he stressed was joy. Now the Ba'al Shem Tov was not naive. He knew about pogroms. He was familiar with what had happened in 1648. He understood that Jewish life was harsh. But the Besht also knew that *kvetching* was really an admission of defeat. And so he challenged Jews to kick their *kvetching* habit.

Once when he was asked what his major teaching was, the Ba'al Shem answered:

It is the aim and essence of my pilgrimage on earth to show members of my community through my own actions, that one may serve God with merriment and rejoicing. For one who is full of joy is full of love for people and for all fellow creatures.

No more guilt, no more fasting, no more beating up the body. A new way of life.

Jewish tradition speaks about "the joy of observing the mitzvot," the divine directives of the Torah. This was true for the Besht, but he went even further—all forms of pleasure, such as eating, drinking, and lovemaking should also be experienced in a joyous manner, with the intentionality that we are serving God.

There is an element of the highest love
  in all of your worldly pleasures,
    and through your natural desires for such delights
      it becomes easy for you to come to the love of God.
If this were not true, how difficult it would be
  for you to even begin to love God!
But, because you are able to arouse such love
  through physical pleasures,
    it becomes easy to love God.
Meditate on this.

And yes, it is true:
Your love for physical pleasures

*is not the highest form of love,
and yet it does derive from the highest love.*

Hasidic tradition asserts that the Ba'al Shem introduced sacred song and dance as joyous communal forms of spiritual practice. He borrowed secular songs from the Polish peasants and may have appropriated their dances as well. Such song and dance drew people to the spirit, but they were also expressions of the soul, intoxicated with holiness.

In one recent collection of tales about the Ba'al Shem, the master explains the power of ecstatic dance for Hasidic men:

When Hasidim are engaged in worship, an explosive spirit swirls within their souls that cleave to the living God. It shakes their body and limbs until the body starts to dance ecstatically, because dances are the body's prayers, on the level of "All my bones shall say, 'Oh Lord, who is like You!' The body and all its limbs dance to the rhythm of the heart, which moves and flows with the prayer of the universe. And the heart feels that its beating is only an echo of the motion of the worlds and that with its beating it embraces those worlds that unite with their Creator and become, so to speak—like the union of male and female—one flesh."

Yitzhak Buxbaum, *The Light and Fire of the Baal Shem Tov*, Continuum, 2005, p. 156

Many teachings attributed to the Besht seem to make sadness and melancholy almost sinful.

> *This is the great tenet in serving the Creator:*
> *Guard yourself from sadness in every possible way,*
>   *for weeping is very bad.*
> *You must serve God in joy.*
> *But if your weeping is occasioned by joy,*
>   *then it is very good.*
> *Sadness frustrates your ability to serve God.*
> *It is so much better for you to serve the Blessed One with joy,*
>   *and without austerities, for they bring about sadness.*

I believe that the extreme form that these teachings took emerged out of a powerful desire to counter the overwhelming weight of sorrow that the Besht and the other early Hasidic teachers found among the people. Historians have shown that there was not a lot of active anti-Semitism during the Besht's lifetime, but the accumulated sorrows of Jewish history, and most especially the trauma of the Chmielnitski massacres of the seventeenth century had most certainly left their mark on the Jewish soul.

What was the meaning of radical joy for the Ba'al Shem Tov? Obviously, it was not the mere enjoyment of life on the physical plane, nor was it "getting high" in a spiritual sense, for such states only make the ego-self feel good for a limited time. Radical joy is a sacred way of cultivating the divine presence, in large measure through appreciation and gratitude. It asks the seeker to open his or her heart to the vast realm of the Spirit. The sense of self expands, opening to a spacious all-embracing state of consciousness. The problems and irritations of physical existence melt in the recognition of the overpowering truth of the miraculous nature of existence. It is this experience of utter freedom and joy that alters one's attitudes and beliefs in a fundamental way, so that even in conditions of outer exile it was still possible for Jews to find their way toward inner spiritual freedom.

But how is it possible to be joyful when one is facing adversity or experiencing suffering? The very question might seem absurd because joy and suffering seem to be complete opposites.

> A man once asked the Ba'al Shem Tov:
> "How can we live in this world with all the suffering we are forced to bear?"
> The master answered:
> "Accept everything that happens to you in this world in the spririt of love, and you will have a good life in both this world and the next."
> "How difficult that would be!" replied the man.
> "Yes, I know. And I pray that you will be able to do this," replied the Besht.

The Besht knew that his advice would be hard to follow, but nevertheless he affirmed that it was indeed possible. When I first encountered this little story I, too, found the Ba'al Shem's counsel somewhat strange.

And then I came across a book by psychologist Barry Neil Kaufman called *Happiness is a Choice*. I must admit that when I first picked up this little paperback, I found the title a bit off-putting and I was skeptical of its contents. Yet in story after story the author demonstrates that our attitudes determine how we respond to difficulty.

Kaufman relates the anecdote of an encounter he had in a class he once taught on developing self-trust. A severely asthmatic man raised his hand with a question. He had gone from doctor to doctor, he was taking all the medication they prescribed, but nothing was really of any help. "I just can't stand it," the man said.

"This may sound silly or crazy or both," Kaufman replied, "but I'll do my best to give you a useful response. Be happy with your asthma! Instead of treating it like an enemy, embrace it like a friend. If you change your attitude about your condition you'll change the chemistry in your body. Every thought we have is a physical event. Neurotransmitters and neuropeptides pop into existence throughout the body each time we activate a belief. Change the belief (the thought, the perspective, the judgment) and we change or, at the very least, influence the physical event we call our 'bodymind.' Your attitude and intelligence exist everywhere in the 50 trillion cells of your body. This is a marvelous and concrete opportunity for you, and not just a pie-in-the-sky game. Give yourself and your asthma a different message and see what happens. So, when you have the tightness in your chest, the shortness of breath, the wheezing and coughing, you could first welcome it, talk to it, even play with it. Then open yourself, ultimately, to loving it . . . really loving it!"

The man was amused, intrigued and skeptical, but he agreed to try Kaufman's advice. The next day he reported that he had followed the approach that Kaufman had suggested. At first he felt ridiculous, "but soon something magically freed up inside and I really felt loving and loved." His eyes filled with tears. "You know, in no time at all, I fell asleep. Right now, I feel more comfortable and peaceful in my body than I have in months."

Barry Neil Kaufman, *Happiness is a Choice,* Fawcett Columbine, N.Y., 1991, pp. 6-7

Kaufman asserts that we can become prisoners of our perspectives, but that we have the power to become the architects of our own attitudes and experiences. "As belief-makers, we can create any vision of the universe we want and then accumulate evidence to support it. In choosing the happiness option, and the attitudinal advantage which flows from it, we open a window to the world that reveals a wonderful and supportive environment …." And, he adds, "In choosing happiness, I have encountered a happy God. In choosing love, I have encountered a loving God."

Over the years I have found truth in Kaufman's radical approach to dealing with pain and adversity, and it has enabled me to understand and appreciate the Ba'al Shem Tov's way of dealing with suffering. As I encounter the infirmities of aging, I try to accept them in love. I'm not always successful in this. I find myself *kvetching*, either to myself or to others. Nonetheless, I continue to try to incorporate the Ba'al Shem's wisdom into my life. When I'm able to do this I find that it does make a great deal of difference.

SWEETENING SUFFERING

Mortality is a problem for us because we don't want to grow old, we don't want to become infirm, we don't want to die. All three of these issues—aging, sickness, and death—have to do with fear and suffering. This theme has a profound personal meaning for me, for there have been times when I have had to face some pretty bleak situations in my life. There have been periods when I've been overwhelmed by confusion or I have disappeared into inner emptiness. I've undergone dark nights of the soul, times when I have been confronted by frightening phantoms from my past, ghosts which tried to catch me up in their curses and often succeeded. There have been days—even recently—when I found myself regressing into negative childhood patterns, and I lost my adult sense of control and responsibility.

If you are at all familiar with Buddhism, you know that the issue of human suffering and the ending of suffering is central to the Buddhist path. In fact, from the Buddha's point of view, suffering is the major catalyst for the journey that leads toward spiritual awakening. The Ba'al Shem Tov, like the Buddha, viewed suffering as an experience that could and should lead an individual toward self-transformation. One of his maxims was: *"Ha'rah hu ki'sei el ha'tov,"* which might be translated, "Adversity is the throne of goodness."

The Ba'al Shem Tov, too, had to face his own dark nights of the soul. When he was just a small child, his father died and apparently his mother disappeared. The community attempted to care for him as he grew up, but he was a willful child and he would often absent himself from school, running away into the woods. When he was sixteen he married, but his young wife died a year later. The Besht may have internalized these tragedies, believing that he was somehow at fault for what had happened, for we are told that in his early years he lived as an ascetic, practicing self-mortification. Somehow, however, he came to see this traditional response to suffering as erroneous. The Besht eventually learned and taught the transformative power of love, pleasure and joy, and spoke against the debilitating dominance of guilt, shame, and morbid rumination over one's sinfulness.

One of the Ba'al Shem Tov's great insights has to do with how an individual can move from suffering and sadness to joy and blessing. I first learned this teaching from one of my teachers, Rabbi Miles Krassen. Reb Miles taught that the Ba'al Shem outlined a three-step process for the transformation of suffering. Here's what the Besht taught:

> *An individual should cultivate three ways of dealing with adversity: Yielding, Discernment, and Sweetening ... .*
> *If you are able to purify your thinking regarding what is good and pleasant about each of the occurrences that*

> *happen to you through Yielding, Discernment and Sweetening . . . you will then be able to hold your footing, and you won't be toppled by the husks of evil. You will remain bound in oneness to the Blessed One.*

I'd like to lay out the Ba'al Shem's process briefly, and then go into some detail about each of the steps.

First of all, the Ba'al Shem counsels the sufferer to enter into the heart of the suffering, into the pain, accepting it fully. The second step has to do with searching in one's suffering for the spark of light that is hidden there. Finally, by concentrating all of one's attention on that spark, and by intensifying its light, the sufferer will eventually be able to dispel the darkness of their adversity.

Now, let's examine each of the steps.

Our culture encourages us to hide or deny the reality of suffering, so that when we meet it head-on we are often totally unprepared. Rabbi Jonathan Magonet has written, "If religion has a task in a secular world, it is to encourage us to accept the reality of suffering, and then to try to move beyond it." So the first step, the Besht taught, is yielding to the reality of one's pain and suffering. When you are caught up in adversity, you must accept your pain fully. This is called *hachna'ah*, yielding or surrender. I can tell you from first-hand experience how difficult this is. No one likes to experience pain. But the problem is this: When we resist our pain, we make it worse; we suffer because we add our resistance to the pain itself. And then we have to deal with the pain of resisting as well as the essential pain itself.

The Besht taught that we have a choice in how we deal with adversity:

> *Through accepting pain in a spirit of joy,*
> *your pain* (TZaRaH) *becomes transformed*
> *into acceptance* (RaTZaH).

Let me offer you an example of this from my own life. In the late 1980s my seven-year marriage began to come apart, but I was oblivious to the signs. When my wife informed me that she was going to file for divorce, I was stunned by her decision, and this opened out into fear and dread as my world began to come apart. And then, only a few months later, my mother died. I'd had a difficult relationship with Mom as a child, but in my adult life she and I had become close friends, sharing a mutual interest in spirituality, the visual arts, culture and politics. I was shaken by losing her, all the more so because it came on the heels of my marital breakup. I had lost the two most important women in my life, and I had fallen into a black hole. I wasn't sure whether or not I would survive. Somehow I needed to accept what was happening, but I didn't know if this was at all possible.

Years before, my spiritual director, Pastor Ted Pecot, had told me that I was too unyielding, and that I needed to learn to abandon myself to God. "I'm willing to abandon myself to God's goodness," I had told him, "but not to God's evil. How can I surrender to the God who allowed the Holocaust to happen?"

"No," he replied, "when you give yourself to God, you abandon *all* of yourself to all of God." I didn't really grasp what he was saying and his proposition seemed impossible to me. If I gave my self to God, what then would be left?

A few years later, Judith Binetter, a good friend from Israel who possessed great insight into the human soul, told me that she experienced me as being overly controlling. "Let go!" she would shout at me in her German accent. "Why do you hold on to this image of yourself? Each moment is different. Each moment unique. Let go of the past and be in the present." But again I didn't really understand what she meant.

The day my wife informed me about the divorce, I called Ted, who offered me his deepest consolation. Then I called Judith in Tel Aviv. She shouted at me over the phone, "Let it go! Let it go, Burt. Don't hold on." I put the phone down. How could she be so callous, I thought, angered by her response. Much later I came to see that Ted had responded as one kind of spiritual director and Judith had reacted as another kind of spiritual director — or perhaps a Zen master! — trying to shock me into accepting the present situation in its fullness, rather than wallowing in self-pity. It took a great deal of time, but slowly the truth of what Judith and Ted had observed and shared with me over the years began to sink in.

I realized that Ted and Judith had both been right: I had attempted to stake my life on a rigid idea of how I thought it needed to be. And I came to recognize that if I were to survive these two losses, I would have to learn to surrender, to yield my wounded ego to God. I was not thinking of the Ba'al Shem Tov at the time. I did not know that he had spoken about these sorts of issues. But my decision to let go was the first step of the Ba'al Shem's three step approach to dealing with adversity: *hachna'ah*.

The second step, the Ba'al Shem taught, is called *havdalah* or Discernment. In the Havdalah ritual ending Shabbat, Jews declare that God "discerns (HaMaVDiL) that which is sacred from that which is profane (or ordinary), light from darkness, etc." According to the Ba'al Shem, *havdalah* is the ability to discern the Light—the presence of the divine in the midst of the misery of our experience.

Discernment is the process of distinguishing the still, small Voice of the Spirit from the cacophony of noises and voices in your life, so that you can listen to it, hear its message and come to understand the spiritual purpose and meaning of your suffering. This voice is always a call to freedom, meaning and joy. To enter the path of transformation, of course, requires a conscious choice. Moses tells the people: "I set before you today the blessing and the curse... Choose life that you and your children may live...." (Deuteronomy 30:19) Discernment is a choice for life that enables the suffering individual to understand what God or the Living Spirit requires of him or her.

So I asked myself: Where was the light hidden in the melancholy of my mother's death and in my divorce? These events, which had broken my heart, forced me to make a decision: I had to change, and in order to change I knew that I had to surrender to God. And this would require my taking on a spiritual discipline. I had not engaged in regular spiritual practice for twenty years, ever since I had left the bounds of traditional

Judaism, but now I began to practice a daily form of meditation in which I simply gave my self over to God. *"B'yad'khah afkid ruchi…."* "Into Your hand I entrust my spirit…." (Psalms 31:6)

The Ba'al Shem's second step may seem a bit like whistling in the dark. But whistling in the dark may be just what is called for. Religious novelist Frederick Buechner wrote that: To whistle in the dark is … . to remind yourself that dark is not all there is, or the end of all there is, because even in the dark there is hope … even in the dark you have the power to whistle. And sometimes that seems more than just your own power because it's powerful enough to hold the dark back a little. The tunes you whistle in the dark are the images you make of that hope, that power … ."

In the summer of 1991 I returned to San Antonio for the unveiling of my mother's gravestone. When I returned to Oakland, the final divorce papers were waiting for me. And then, two weeks later a firestorm swept through the Oakland and Berkeley hills. Hundreds of homes were destroyed, including the house I lived in, and virtually all of my belongings went up in smoke. Yet this immense destruction did not affect me emotionally. The loss of the two people closest to me loomed so much larger than the loss of mere possessions.

More important, I had already begun to surrender my life and destiny to the divine. I came to see the fire as a kind of testing: How far had I come in learning to yield? The months after the fire were difficult, but I was not shattered. After all, I was alive and no one that I knew had been killed. I had lost only possessions. For me, the discovery that I needed to yield my life to the Spirit through meditation became the second step of the

Ba'al Shem's three-step process.

And so we come to the Besht's third step, which he calls *ham'ta'kah* or Sweetening. When we are living with tension and then that tension is released, we come into joy and delight. In like manner, for the Besht, *havdalah* (discernment) leads to *ham'ta'kah* (the sweetening of our lives). The energy we have heretofore placed into identification with our adversity and with our suffering can now be released and transformed into joy. This sweetening may not always affect the physical conditions of adversity that impinge upon our lives. We may still find ourselves in a painful situation. But our act of *havdalah* has brought about an inward change, and we are now able to cope with the external difficulties out of an inner sense of resolution, freedom and joy. In like manner, Buddhists teach that the pain itself may not dissipate, but the suffering will.

In my own case my practice of meditation has had important effects on my life over the past twenty-five years. While meditating I often experience the divinity of all things. The practice has taught me humility. More and more I realize that I am just a small finite part of a vast universe, privileged to live on this planet for a short time; but at my core there is something infinite, which is my true identity. I have come to accept my gifts and my greatness as a human being as a single instance of divine grace. The practice has also given me a great deal more calm, acceptance, and equanimity. Because of this I'm better able to witness myself screwing up without always getting caught up in the screw-ups.

There are times in my life when I experience difficult

crises, when I have to struggle with negative inner patterns. The old ghosts don't give up easily. Over and over again I have had to re-learn the necessity of surrender. Almost every day I experience resistance as I engage in my meditative practice. Yet, I know that because of my practice I have grown, and so I persist.

TEACHER OF ENLIGHTENMENT

Of all the ways in which the Ba'al Shem Tov served his community I am most fascinated by his devotion to his disciples as a teacher of enlightenment. I believe that the master's utterances, recorded by his disciples, were primarily aimed at enabling them to transform themselves into *hasidim*, godly individuals who would then be able to contribute to the eventual messianic transformation of the Jewish people and the world. To the Besht, personal transformation (*tikkun ha'nefesh*) was a necessary prerequisite to world transformation (*tikkun ha'olam*).

Years ago I wondered how I might best encapsulate the Besht's path to liberation in words. I was somewhat familiar with Buddhism and so I turned to the Buddha's teachings as a kind of template for shaping my understanding of the Ba'al Shem's path to enlightenment. The Buddha divided his approach into Four Noble Truths and Eight Noble Pathways to achieve those fundamental truths. So I began to examine the teachings of the Besht, seeking to delineate the major truths and the pathways toward those truths. I did not seek to imitate the Buddha's Four Noble Truths, but inspired by the Buddha, I sought to extract from the mass of teachings and stories the essential teachings of the Besht so they might become accessible to contemporary seekers.

The task turned out to be far more difficult than I had imagined. I examined hundreds of texts, and as far as I could tell, the Ba'al Shem Tov had not provided his students with a simple and comprehensive statement that embodied his full understanding of what it would mean to be a *hasid*. His insights, as they have come down to us, are not organized in a linear manner, nor are the teachings entirely consistent with one another. Time after time my attempts at systematic formulation failed. I came to feel that his thought was simply too rich and varied to be reduced and simplified. Unlike the Buddha, the Besht was not only fashioning a new spiritual path for individual seekers. He was also re-envisioning the entirety of Judaism through the lens of his mystical experience.

Nonetheless, I did not give up my quest. I felt that expressing the master's insights in a simple, linear way could be extremely useful for those—like myself— who view the Besht as a teacher of liberation. More recently, I decided that to accomplish my goal I would have to step into the realm of imagination, filling in the gaps in our knowledge about the Besht's path with my own speculations regarding the process he might have undergone and the discoveries he made that led him to become the amazing teacher he ultimately became.

I cannot, in all honesty, assert that the four truths delineated below represent the fundamental principles of the historical Besht's teaching. What I can say is that of all the truths recorded by the disciples about their master's teachings, these speak most deeply to me, and, I believe, can speak to the hearts and minds of contemporary seekers.

Here, then, is my current version of the Besht's four major truths. Readers interested in this topic can find out more about it in my book, *There is Only One Love: The Ba'al Shem Tov in the Modern World*, Chapters 12 and 13.

THE FOUR GREAT TRUTHS

FIRST TRUTH:
Human life is precarious and transient.
Suffering is unavoidable and inevitable.

The Ba'al Shem recognized that life could be harsh and difficult to endure. He understood how the difficulties and troubles that the people he served contended with—anti-Semitism, violence, poverty, disease, aging and the inevitability of death—could make people's lives unhappy.

The kabbalists who lived before the Besht had also grappled with this issue and had taught that during the process of the creation of the universe an unexpected shattering had destroyed the divine dream of a perfect world. As a result the physical realm in which we live is cut off from the higher, more transcendent realm of divinity. This, according to the Besht, is at the root of all the conflict in the world. Most people live with a very partial and warped understanding of existence. They identify their own views with truth and they see the views of others as distorted.

The Ba'al Shem saw the effect that all this hardship was having on his people's lives. Individuals were cut off from empathizing with one another, and they felt distant from God. He knew that many Jews performed their religious duties without spiritual passion. He also understood how, in the face of such conditions, there were those who turned their attention to personal fulfillment rather than to the religious life. But he was also aware of how the negativity and doubt that he encountered among Jews was falsely anchored in evidence presented by the senses and the mind alone. Without a deep experience of and faith in that which transcends physical reality, we become lost.

SECOND TRUTH:
Life surprises us with wonder and joy,
summoning us toward transcendence.

The Ba'al Shem knew that even though people's lives were challenging, life was not entirely painful. The Sabbath and the holy days open the heart to joy. And human life is punctuated by "ordinary" moments of grace, times of pleasure, joy, and humor. Through these we become aware of the wonder, majesty, and mystery of the world—the birth of a child, the joy of a couple sharing their love for one another, a gorgeous mountain or ocean vista, a colorful flower opening to the sun, a delicate hummingbird sipping from a feeder. Or we might meet a deeply realized individual, someone who exhibits unconditional love and goodness.

Somewhere, deep inside, we realize that there is more to

this life than the happiness that continually slips away and the harshness of existence on this earth. We know that we are more than our material bodies.

Experiences of wonderment and radical amazement have the potential of opening the heart to a deep sense of gratitude and joy, the recognition that despite all of its adversity life is precious and worthwhile. These experiences are invitations to transcendence. They arouse our desire to delve more deeply into the realm of the spirit.

THIRD TRUTH:
Through faith in and attachment to the divine, through spiritual practice, and through personal effort we can transform our lives so that we become lovers of God and everything that God created. We have the ability to transform life on earth.

However marvelous, our senses and our minds are not the only avenues to truth, and they can actually mislead us as we seek a greater, more transcendent reality. Through ecstatic mystical worship the Besht came to an awareness of a pristine mystical oneness at the very heart of reality that transcended the brokenness of life. When he gave himself to this larger, ineffable state of awareness he was able to experience the love that permeates the entirety of existence.

As he learned how to inhabit this larger state of consciousness, it became evident to the Besht that without the constant flow of the life force into the world nothing at all would exist. He knew that human beings have been graced with souls that allow them to intuit the presence of the Infinite within the finite.

The Ba'al Shem discovered that the insights he experienced through his intuition and imagination opened his heart and mind to a greater reality. All this led him to perceive physical reality as a radiation of the actual presence of the Spirit. He knew that the kabbalists had been correct: "There is no place devoid of the divine." The mystery we call God is at the heart of the holy and the ordinary alike, and can be found in both good and evil.

With the recognition that divinity is streaming through everything comes the understanding that even our adversity is permeated with divine concern. And because God is present in our suffering, we can sweeten it and possibly transform it into love and joy.

Nonetheless, the master realized that there were mysteries too deep to be fathomed by the human mind and that in the end existence is a riddle that cannot be solved.

Through the years the Besht came to realize his own divine essence and he gradually shed his limiting attachment to his ego and his self-serving desires. Nonetheless he knew that desire itself was holy, for it could lead the seeker to the Origin of desire.

The master experienced a supreme joy, recognizing that he and all others are loved by God and that the primary responsibility we have as human beings and as Jews is to love God and all of God's creations in return.

He knew that every person had a spark of the messiah within and that through our actions we can contribute to sweetening and healing the harshness and suffering of the world by revealing the goodness at its root.

FOURTH TRUTH:

The realization of enlightenment requires ongoing spiritual dedication and engagement, guided by the Ten Pathways to Transformation.

The Ba'al Shem taught his disciples that they had a choice. They could look at the world with eyes of fear, focusing on evil and suffering. Or they could look at the world with eyes of love, centering on goodness and joy. He knew that there was truth in both of these paths, but he was convinced that it was the duty of the aspiring *hasid* to learn to see with eyes of love, devoting oneself to illuminating despondency and bringing love, compassion and joy to others.

His disciples were traditional Jews who observed the full range of *mitzvot* (deeds which united people with God and God's creations), and they cultivated certain *middot* (ethical and spiritual virtues) in depth. And the master encouraged each of them to evolve their own particular way of hasidic living and serving.

He taught his disciples that there were ten pathways to transformation. His followers discovered that by attaching themselves to their master's vision and learning his pathways to enlightenment they could approach their Jewish heritage in a radically new way.

Ecstatic prayer became the center of their lives. The study of Torah came alive for them in transformative ways. The observance of the *mitzvot* with spiritual intentionality brought renewed vigor to their souls. The new Hasidic spiritual practices introduced by their teacher freed them to access their deeper potential. God became a living force in their lives. And their love for God, Torah and the Jewish people deepened.

THE TEN PATHWAYS

1. CHANNELING TORAH

The Ba'al Shem taught his disciples that they should not study Torah merely for the sake of gaining knowledge. He urged them to deepen their recognition of the divine character of their minds. He taught them to cultivate their intuition and their imagination in the service of true wisdom and understanding. Through this process they were able to link themselves with the Torah in a way that unveiled novel hidden truths relevant to their spiritual advancement.

2. WORSHIPPING IN ECSTASY

The Besht recognized that mystical prayer can lift the consciousness of the worshipper to realms that neither intellect nor intuition can reach. He urged them to learn to let go, to lose themselves in the Beloved, to disappear into the darkness that is all light. In this way they rooted themselves in the oneness and mystery of the divine, and their vision was renewed again and again.

3. ENGAGING IN JOYOUS SERVICE

The master taught that joy is the very heart of religious living, the essence of faith, greater than all other religious virtues. He taught them to bring a sense of gratitude to all of their forms of serving God and people. Such gratefulness required them to consciously turn their attention away from what they perceived was missing from their lives and instead to focus their attention on the appreciation of the abundant gifts that they were regularly receiving from God.

4. SWEETENING SUFFERING

The Besht taught his students that because there is no place devoid of the divine, God could be found through their suffering as well as through their joy.

He offered them a three-part process for dealing with adversity: Surrender to adversity, Discernment of the presence of God in the adversity, and Sweetening Suffering.

5. CULTIVATING AWE AND LOVE

People tend to make their egos and their personal desires into guideposts for how they navigate their lives. As a result their lives circle around themselves and lack a sense of transcendence, reverence and affection for God and God's creations. The Ba'al Shem taught that in order to truly serve God people need to develop or deepen their sense of awe and love for existence and for its Origin. He proclaimed that to be a *hasid* was to be in love with God and with what God created.

6. UNIFYING MATTER AND SPIRIT, BODY AND SOUL

The Besht taught his students that relationships, sexuality, eating, work, errands, and recreation were all necessary components of their daily lives. These activities might not always seem to have a spiritual dimension, but since there is no place devoid of the divine, any and all of these relationships and actions could become entrances into holiness. But this depends on intentionality. If a seeker consciously cultivates a more expanded state of consciousness while he is carrying out each of his deeds, he could then elevate his deeds and provide deeper meaning for his existence.

7. SEEKING INWARDNESS IN ONE'S SACRED DEEDS

The master taught that a *mitzvah* is not merely an action dictated by God. Each and every *mitzvah* has the power to unite the individual with the divine. But this doesn't happen automatically. Seekers need to bring their full intentionality and will to every deed they engage in.

8. TRANSFORMING EVIL

The Besht told his disciples that God wishes to be served by the entire self, by the evil as well as by the good impulse. This means that they had to learn how to transform their self-serving impulses so that through them they would be able to serve the good. He taught them to uplift their drives and passions, transforming them into ways of serving God and others.

9. LIVING IN THE PRESENCE

The Besht understood that the ordinary activities that people engage in throughout the day often fragment their consciousness and draw them away from remembering that each moment is precious and that they are part of the totality of being. He taught them to recognize that creation is filled with God's Presence (the *Shekhinah*), and therefore there is neither place nor moment that cannot become an opening in which the seeker might encounter the divine.

10. GROWING IN HUMILITY AND SIMPLICITY

The Ba'al Shem emphasized the notion that all human abilities, talents and accomplishments come from the power of divinity that moves through and energizes our lives. He told his students that their individual gifts could only help redeem the fallen world as long as they remembered to be humble, recognizing that they were small parts of the greater whole. He linked humility with simplicity, teaching the importance of purity of heart, uncomplicated by the turmoil of the mind that would keep them from wholehearted openness to people, to nature and to God.

CONCLUSION

Love was scarce in my family of origin, and the great challenge of my life has been learning how to love—to love people, to love life, to love God. When I first encountered the Ba'al Shem Tov, I sensed that he would be a spiritual teacher who could guide me in my quest. I read stories about the Besht's life. I studied his teachings. I created spiritual practices for myself that were inspired by the Besht's own teachings and practices. I engaged in work with my spiritual director using teachings of the Besht. And I taught classes about the Besht.

All of this has had a positive effect on my own personal development. I have become increasingly aware of the loving presence of the divine flowing through all things. The Ba'al Shem's vision helped me work on negative traits that had stunted me from childhood. My capacity to care for people and the world has grown. I have internalized many of my teacher's insights regarding compassion, gratitude, joy, ecstasy, surrender, equanimity and liberation. There are times when I lose my footing and slip up, sometimes badly, and I know that I must continue to work to deepen the spiritual and moral qualities that I have learned from the Besht.

Although the Ba'al Shem Tov has been essential to my personal spiritual development, I have also had to attend to psychological issues stemming from a dysfunctional childhood, and I have benefited immensely from psychotherapy. Spiritual direction has also been essential to my inner growth, offering me ways to understand both the spiritual dimension and the spiritual direction of my experience.

So, you may ask, have I achieved what I was searching for? Am I spiritually free? I often experience inner freedom when I am meditating or *davening* (worshipping). It is then that I can let go into the whole of existence and the mystery at its depths. Through such spiritual practice I can experience exaltation, ecstasy, love, oneness, surrender—all manifestations of the divine presence.

And when I meet adversity in my daily life—my own or someone else's—I'm often able to mitigate its effect on me by recognizing that this anguish is truly a part of the entire fabric of existence, and that God is present in suffering just as God is present in all experience. As the Ba'al Shem taught, "When you recognize that God is with you, then the sorrow dissipates." Just knowing this decreases the amount of suffering I need to endure.

I believe that all of my inner struggles have made me a deeper, more loving human being. Most of the time I am no longer subject to the power of the negative patterns that dominated my life as a young man. In all candor, however, I have to admit that my search for the kind of enlightenment and spiritual perfection I had pursued for so long has failed. I have remained fully human, still contending with self-centeredness, still learning how to love and to serve.

Yet the Ba'al Shem Tov taught me not to be too hard on myself. One time, reading a verse from the biblical book of Ecclesiastes, "There is no righteous man *(tzaddik)* on earth who does only good and does not sin" (7:20), he commented, "One cannot continually remain in a state of goodness in which one has no negative motivations or sins. This is impossible!" On another occasion he told his disciples:

> *The work of a human being in this world is to struggle time after time—until his very last breath—with that which is foreign to his spirit, and time after time to integrate the foreign into the very essence of the Holy Name, may it be blessed.*

I have found that my imperfections provide an incentive to live in greater humility. I now know that the brokenness that I suffered as a child was just one instance of the larger brokenness of the world, that which the Besht called "the exile of the *Shekhinah*." The gift of this brokenness is compassion for all those who are broken. And I have come to see that despite the inevitable difficulties and suffering that are part of living, my existence is a gift of the Infinite.

For Judaism the Besht's Torah represented a new beginning, a major paradigm shift, a movement away from a religion primarily defined by obligation to what I would call a spirituality of exaltation, love and human enhancement.

ACKNOWLEDGEMENTS

I have been toiling for decades on two rather large manuscripts having to do with the life and teachings of Israel Ba'al Shem Tov. A few years ago, my friend, Rabbi Lawrence Kushner, suggested that I write a short accessible book about the Besht's primary teachings. I want to thank Larry for planting the seed that eventually became this book.

Each Yom Kippur afternoon since 2008 I have been offering my congregants at Kehilla Community Synagogue a short teaching drawn from the life and thought of the Besht. As my eightieth birthday—also my fiftieth year as a rabbi—was approaching in 2016 my wife, Rabbi Diane Elliot, suggested that I might collect and edit these short talks into a small book. To give readers a fuller sense of the Besht's contribution to Jewish life I added four new pieces, the Introduction, Chapters 1 and 8, and the Conclusion. The result is *This Precious Moment*.

The anecdotes and stories about the Besht found in this book come from a variety of sources. The teachings of the Besht that I have gathered over many years are highlighted in this book by indenting and italicizing them. The major sources for these teachings are *Me'ir Einei Yisrael: Torat Ha'Ba'al Shem Tov*, edited by Yehoshua Yosef Kornbleit (Machon Da'at Yosef, Jerusalem, 5751) and *B'er Ha'hasidut: Sefer HaBesht*, by Eliezer Steinmann (Machon L'ho'tza'at Kabbalah, Macha'shavah, Hasidut). The quotes are my own translations from the Hebrew. Several of the stories come from *Shiv'hei HaBesht*, the earliest collection of tales about the Besht.

My thanks go to Richard Stone, Rabbi Cynthia Hoffman, Stuart Jacobson and Rabbi Dev Noily for their support and suggestions. Many thanks to my wife, Rabbi Diane Elliot, for her skillful editing.

Special thanks to Don Stone for his detailed proofreading. And heartfelt appreciation to Richard Miles for designing the book and for all of his labor at getting it into print.

El Sobrante, California
September 2016

www.ingramcontent.com/pod-product-compliance
Lightning Source LLC
Chambersburg PA
CBHW051955290426
44110CB00015B/2256